The Catholic Book of Prayer

Rene Prescott

Contents

From the Author

"Prayer is an aspiration of the heart, it is a simple glance directed to heaven, it is a cry of gratitude and love in the midst of trail as well as joy; finally, it is something great, supernatural, which expands my soul and unites me to Jesus." - St.Therese of Lisieux

Many years ago when I was growing up, a relative gave me a little book of Catholic prayers. It was a simple book, with no pictures, and for most children that would probably not have been very exciting. I wasn't most children though and I loved that book. I carried it with me everywhere I went; to school, mass, even when I was out playing I would have the book stuffed in a pocket, in my backpack or somewhere close to hand.

A few years ago I scoured the web looking for the book. While I did eventually find it, the book had sadly been out of print for years. The book wasn't for me, I was planning on giving it away as a gift and so rather than give up on my quest I decided to write a book of my own.

I spent countless hours at the local library, digging through traditional Catholic prayers. I researched the saints, their lives and the prayers they left for us. I spent time on religious forums, chatting with other Catholics and I spent even longer, reflecting and thinking back to the prayers I was taught to pray when I was a child.

The result of all that work is this: The Catholic Book of Prayer. It's a simple book just like the one I once had but it's a powerful book. One, thanks to the digital world we live in today, that you can take anywhere and one that will, hopefully, give you the same joy, peace and faith that my little book of Catholic prayers gave me all those years ago.

Thank you for reading the book and do please pass on any criticisms, comments or questions to me.

Rene Prescott

"Prayer is the raising of one's mind and heart to God or the requesting of good things from God"

St. John Damascene

Common Prayers

"Pray as though everything depended on God. Work as though everything depended on you."
- St. Augustine

Our Father

Our Father, Who art in heaven,
Hallowed be Thy Name.
Thy Kingdom come.
Thy Will be done, on earth as it is in Heaven.
Give us this day our daily bread.
And forgive us our trespasses,
as we forgive those who trespass against us.
And lead us not into temptation,
but deliver us from evil.
Amen.

Sign of the Cross

In the name of the Father,
and of the Son,
and of the Holy Spirit.
Amen.

Glory Be

Glory be to the Father,
and to the Son,
and to the Holy Spirit.
As it was in the beginning,
is now,
and ever shall be,
world without end.
Amen.

Apostles' Creed

I believe in God, the Father Almighty, Creator of Heaven and earth;
and in Jesus Christ, His only Son Our Lord,
Who was conceived by the Holy Spirit, born of the Virgin Mary,
suffered under Pontius Pilate, was crucified, died, and was buried.
He descended into Hell; the third day He rose again from the dead;
He ascended into Heaven, and sitteth at the right hand of God, the Father almighty;
from thence He shall come to judge the living and the dead.
I believe in the Holy Spirit, the holy Catholic Church, the communion of saints,
the forgiveness of sins, the resurrection of the body and life everlasting.
Amen.

Nicene Creed

We believe in one God, the Father, the Almighty,
maker of heaven and earth, of all that is seen and unseen.
We believe in one Lord, Jesus Christ, the only Son of God,
eternally begotten of the Father,
God from God, Light from Light, true God from true God,
begotten, not made, one in Being with the Father.
Through him all things were made.
For us men and for our salvation he came down from heaven:
by the power of the Holy Spirit he was born of the Virgin Mary, and
became man.
For our sake he was crucified under Pontius Pilate; he suffered, died, and
was buried.
On the third day he rose again in fulfillment of the Scriptures;
he ascended into heaven and is seated at the right hand of the Father.
He will come again in glory to judge the living and the dead,
and his kingdom will have no end.
We believe in the Holy Spirit, the Lord, the giver of life, who proceeds
from the Father and the Son.
With the Father and the Son he is worshipped and glorified.
He has spoken through the Prophets.
We believe in one holy catholic and apostolic Church.
We acknowledge one baptism for the forgiveness of sins.
We look for the resurrection of the dead, and the life of the world to come.
Amen.

The Serenity Prayer

God grant me the serenity to accept the things I cannot change
The courage to change the things I can
And the wisdom to know the difference
Living one day at a time
Enjoying one moment at a time
Accepting hardships as the pathway to peace
Taking, as God did, this sinful world as it is,
Not as I would have it
Trusting that God will make all things right
If I surrender to God's will
That I may be reasonably happy in this life,
And supremely happy with God forever in the next.
Amen.

The Confiteor

I confess to almighty God,
to blessed Mary, ever virgin,
to blessed Michael the archangel,
to blessed John the Baptist,
to the holy apostles Peter and Paul
and to all the saints that I have sinned exceedingly in thought, word and
deed,
through my fault, through my fault, through my most grievous fault.
Therefore I beseech blessed Mary, ever virgin,
blessed Michael the archangel,
blessed John the Baptist,
the holy apostles Peter and Paul
and all the saints to pray to the Lord our God for me.
May almighty God have mercy on us,
forgive us our sins and bring us to everlasting life.
Amen.

Act of Contrition

O my God,
I am heartily sorry for having offended Thee,
and I detest all my sins because I dread the loss of Heaven and the pains of
Hell;
but most of all because they offend Thee, my God,
Who art all-good and deserving of all my love.
I firmly resolve,
with the help of Thy grace,
to confess my sins,
to do penance,
and to amend my life.
Amen.

Divine Praises

Blessed be God.
Blessed be his holy name.
Blessed be Jesus Christ, true God and true man.
Blessed be the name of Jesus.
Blessed be his most Sacred Heart.
Blessed be his most Precious Blood.
Blessed be Jesus in the most holy sacrament of the altar.
Blessed be the Holy Spirit, the Paraclete.
Blessed be the great Mother of God, Mary most holy.
Blessed be her holy and Immaculate Conception.
Blessed be her glorious Assumption.
Blessed be the name of Mary, virgin and Mother.
Blessed be St. Joseph, the most chaste spouse.
Blessed be God in his angels and in his saints.
Amen.

Morning Prayers

Offering of Self

Receive, O Lord, all my liberty.
Take my memory, my understanding and my will.
Whatever I have, whatever I possess You have given to me.
I restore it all to You.
I yield it to be ruled directly by Your will.
Give me only Your love and Your grace and I am rich enough nor do I ask
for more.
Amen.

The Morning Offering

O my God, in union with the Immaculate Heart of Mary
[now you should kiss your Scapular as sign of your consecration to Mary,
which carries a partial indulgence],
I offer Thee the Precious
Blood of Jesus from all the altars throughout the world, joining
with It the offering of my every thought, word and action of this day.
O my Jesus, I desire to day to gain every indulgence and merit
I can and I offer them, together with myself, to Mary Immaculate,
that she may best apply them in the interests of They Most
Sacred Heart. Precious Blood of Jesus, save us!
Immaculate Heart of Mary, pray for us!
Sacred Heart of Jesus, have mercy on us!
Amen.

Act of Faith

O my God,
I firmly believe that you are one God in three divine persons,
Father, Son and Holy Spirit.
I believe that your divine Son became man and died for our sins,
and that he will come to judge the living and the dead.
I believe these and all the truths which the holy catholic Church teaches,
because in revealing them you can neither deceive nor be deceived.
Amen.

Act of Hope

O my God,
relying on Thy almighty power and infinite mercy and promises,
I hope to obtain pardon of my sins,
the help of Thy grace,
and Life Everlasting,
through the merits of Jesus Christ,
my Lord and Redeemer.
Amen.

Act of Love

O My God,
I love you above all things,
with my whole heart and soul,
because you are all-good and worthy of all love.
I love my neighbor as myself for the love of you.
I forgive all who have injured me,
and ask pardon of all whom I have injured.

Act of Charity

O my God,
I love Thee above all things,
with my whole heart and soul,
because Thou art all-good and worthy of all love.
I love my neighbor as myself for the love of Thee.
I forgive all who have injured me,
and ask pardon of all whom I have injured.
Amen.

Family Prayer

"You pay God a compliment by asking great things of Him."

- St. Teresa of Avila

Grace Before Meals

Bless us, O Lord, and these Thy gifts,
which we are about to receive from Thy bounty,
through Christ our Lord.
Amen.

Grace After Meals

We give Thee thanks for all Thy benefits, O Almighty God,
who livest and reignest world without end.
Amen.
May the souls of the faithful departed,
through the mercy of God,
rest in peace.
Amen.

Prayer at Bedtime

Heavenly Father,
Thank you for the day you gave to us.
Please bless (insert name) and keep him/her in your love and protection.
Grant him/her a good night's sleep tonight and send your guardian angels
to watch over him/her while he/she sleeps.
In the name of the Father, and the Son, and of the Holy Spirit.
Amen.

Guardian Angel Prayer

Angel of God,
my guardian dear,
To whom God's love
commits me here,
Ever this day,
be at my side,
To light and guard,
Rule and guide.
Amen.

"For me prayer is a surge of the heart, it is a simple look towards Heaven, it is a cry of recognition and of love, embracing both trial and joy."

- Saint Therese of Lisieux

Prayers to Jesus

"Virtues are formed by prayer. Prayer preserves temperance. Prayer suppresses anger. Prayer prevents emotions of pride and envy. Prayer draws into the soul the Holy Spirit, and raises man to Heaven."

- Saint Ephraem of Syria

Anima Christi

Soul of Christ, make me holy
Body of Christ, be my salvation
Blood of Christ, let me drink your wine
Water flowing from the side of Christ, wash me clean
Passion of Christ, strengthen me
Kind Jesus, hear my prayer
Hide me within your wounds
And keep me close to you
Defend me from the evil enemy
And call me at the hour of my death
To the fellowship of your saints
That I might sing your praise with them
for all eternity.
Amen.

O My Jesus (Fatima)

O my Jesus, forgive us our sins,
save us from the fires of hell;
lead all souls to heaven especially those who are in most need of Your
mercy.
Amen.

An Act of Contrition

O my God,
I am heartily sorry for
having offended Thee,
and I detest all my sins,
because I dread the loss of heaven,
and the pains of hell;
but most of all because
they offend Thee, my God,
Who are all good and
deserving of all my love.
I firmly resolve,
with the help of Thy grace,
to confess my sins,
to do penance,
and to amend my life.
Amen.

Prayer Before a Crucifix

Look down upon me, good and gentle Jesus,
while before Your face I humbly kneel,
and with burning soul pray and beseech You to fix deep in my heart lively
sentiments of faith, hope, and charity,
true contrition for my sins, and a firm purpose of amendment;
while I contemplate with great love and tender pity Your five wounds,
pondering over them within me,
and calling to mind the words which, long ago, David the prophet spoke in
Your own person concerning You, my Jesus:
"They have pierced My hands and My feet; they have numbered all My
bones."

Prayers to Our Lady

"Prayer is the place of refuge for every worry, a foundation for cheerfulness, a source of constant happiness, a protection against sadness."

- St. John Chrysostom

Hail Mary

Hail Mary, full of grace. The Lord is with thee.
Blessed art thou amongst women,
and blessed is the fruit of thy womb, Jesus.
Holy Mary, Mother of God,
pray for us sinners,
now and at the hour of our death.
Amen.

The Angelus

V. The Angel of the Lord declared unto Mary.
R. And she conceived by the Holy Spirit. [Recite the Hail Mary]

V. Behold the handmaid of the Lord.
R. Be it done unto me according to Thy word. [Recite the Hail Mary]

V. And the Word was made flesh.
R. And dwelt among us. [Recite the Hail Mary]

V. Pray for us, O Holy Mother of God.
R. That we may be made worthy of the promises of Christ.

[THE HAIL MARY]

Hail Mary, full of grace, the Lord is with thee.
Blessed art thou among women, and blessed is
the fruit of thy womb, Jesus.
Holy Mary, Mother of God, pray for us sinners,
now, and at the hour of our death. Amen.

LET US PRAY:

Pour forth, we beseech Thee, O Lord, Thy grace into our hearts;
that we to whom the Incarnation of Christ, Thy Son, was made known by
the
message of an Angel, may by His Passion and Cross, be brought to the
glory
of His Resurrection through the same Christ Our Lord. Amen.

Miraculous Medal Prayer

O Mary, conceived without sin,
pray for us who have recourse to thee,
and for those who do not have recourse to thee,
especially the enemies of the Church and those recommended to thee.
Amen.

Act of Reparation to the Immaculate Heart of Mary

O Most Holy Virgin Mother, we listen with grief to the complaints of your Immaculate Heart surrounded with the thorns placed therein at every moment by the blasphemies and ingratitude of ungrateful humanity. We are moved by the ardent desire of loving you as Our Mother and of promoting a true devotion to your Immaculate Heart.

We therefore kneel before you to manifest the sorrow we feel for the grievances that people cause you, and to atone by our prayers and sacrifices for the offenses with which they return return your love.
Obtain for them and for us the pardon of so many sins. Hasten the conversion of sinners that they may love Jesus and cease to offend the Lord, already so much offended.

Turn your eyes of mercy toward us, that we may love God with all our heart on earth and enjoy Him forever in heaven.

Amen

Hail Holy Queen

Hail, Holy Queen, Mother of mercy,
our life, our sweetness and our hope.
To thee do we cry, poor banished children of Eve:
to thee do we send up our sighs,
mourning and weeping in this valley of tears.
Turn then, most gracious Advocate,
thine eyes of mercy toward us,
and after this our exile,
show unto us the blessed fruit of thy womb, Jesus.
O clement, O loving, O sweet Virgin Mary!
Amen.

Memorare

Remember, O most gracious Virgin Mary,
that never was it known
that anyone who fled to thy protection,
implored thy help
or sought thy intercession,
was left unaided.
Inspired by this confidence,
We fly unto thee, O Virgin of virgins my Mother;
to thee do we come, before thee we stand, sinful and sorrowful;
O Mother of the Word Incarnate,
despise not our petitions,
but in thy mercy hear and answer them.
Amen.

The Regina Coeli (for Easter time)

Queen of heaven, rejoice!. Alleluia.
For he whom you did merit to bear. Alleluia.
Has risen, as he said. Alleluia.
Pray for us to God. Alleluia.
Rejoice and be glad, O Virgin Mary, Alleluia.
For the Lord is truly risen. Alleluia.
Let us pray. O God, who gave joy to the world through the resurrection
of your Son our Lord Jesus Christ, grant, we beseech you, that through
the intercession of the virgin Mary, his Mother, we may obtain the joys
of everlasting life, through the same Christ our Lord.
Amen.

The Rosary

"He who prays most receives most."
- St. Alphonsus Maria de Liguori

Purpose of the Rosary

The reason we pray the rosary is to remind ourselves of the suffering Christ endured and the main events that make up our salvation. In doing so, we also praise God for them.

In total there are twenty mysteries to be reflected on when praying the rosary and these are divided into four sections:

- The five "Joyful Mysteries"
- The five "Luminous Mysteries"
- The five "Sorrowful Mysteries"
- The five "Glorious Mysteries"

The groups are prayed on different days:

On Monday and Saturday, meditate on the "Joyful Mysteries"

- First Decade: The Annunciation (Luke 1:26-38)
- Second Decade: The Visitation (Luke 1:39-56)
- Third Decade: The Birth of Our Lord (Luke 2:1-21)
- Fourth Decade: The Presentation (Luke 2:22-38)
- Fifth Decade: The Finding of Our Lord in the Temple (Luke 2:41-52)

On Thursday, meditate on the "Luminous Mysteries"

- First Decade: The Baptism of Our Lord (Matthew 3:13-16)
- Second Decade: The Wedding at Cana (Jn 2:1-11)
- Third Decade: The Proclamation of the Kingdom of God (Mark 1:14-15)
- Fourth Decade: The Transfiguration (Matthew 17:1-8)
- Fifth Decade: The Last Supper, when Our Lord gave us the Holy Eucharist (Mt 26)

On Tuesday and Friday, meditate on the "Sorrowful Mysteries"

- First Decade: The Agony in the Garden (Matthew 26:36-56)
- Second Decade: Our Lord is Scourged at the Pillar (Matthew

27:26)

- Third Decade: Our Lord is Crowned with Thorns (Matthew 27:27-31)
  - Fourth Decade: Our Lord Carries the Cross (Matthew 27:32)
    - Fifth Decade: The Crucifixion (Matthew 27:33-56)

On Wednesday and Sunday, meditate on the "Glorious Mysteries"

- First Decade: The Glorious Resurrection (John 20:1-29)
  - Second Decade: The Ascension (Luke 24:36-53)
- Third Decade: The Descent of the Holy Spirit (Acts 2:1-41)
  - Fourth Decade: The Assumption of Mary into Heaven
- Fifth Decade: The Coronation of Mary as Queen of Heaven and Earth

Steps to Praying the Rosary

First steps...

1. Make the sign of the cross (while holding the crucifix)
2. Say the "Apostles' Creed" (still holding the crucifix)
3. Say the "Our Father" (whilst holding the first large bead)
4. Say three "Hail Marys" (on each of the next small beads)
5. Say the "Glory Be" (on the next large bead)

Second steps...

6. Announce the first mystery (of the group that you're praying that day), then say the "Our Father" (holding the large bead)
7. Say ten "Hail Marys" while meditating on this mystery. (moving along each of the next ten small beads)
8. Say the "Glory be" (holding the next large bead)
9. Announce the second mystery, say the "Our Father", ten "Hail Marys" and the "Glory Be".
10. Continue and repeat these steps saying the remaining mysteries in this manner.
11. After completing all of the mysteries, recite the "Hail, Holy Queen".

Prayer before the Rosary

Queen of the Holy Rosary you have deigned to come to Fatima to reveal to the three shepherd children the treasures of grace hidden in the Rosary.
Inspire my heart with a sincere love of this devotion,
in order that by meditating on the Mysteries of our Redemption which are recalled in it,
I may be enriched with its fruits and obtain peace for the world,
the conversion of sinners and of Russia (and China),
and the favor which I ask you in this Rosary (here mention your request) I ask this for the greater glory of God, for your own honor, and for the good of all souls, especially of my own. Amen.

To Be Said After Each Mystery's Decade

Prayer after the Rosary

O God,
whose only-begotten Son,
by His life, death and resurrection,
has purchased for us the rewards of eternal life;
grant, we beseech Thee, that,
meditating upon these mysteries of the Most Holy Rosary of the Blessed Virgin Mary,
we may imitate what they contain and obtain what they promise through the same Christ our Lord.
Amen.

Prayers for Mass

"My little children, your hearts, are small, but prayer stretches them and makes them capable of loving God. Through prayer we receive a foretaste of heaven and something of paradise comes down upon us. Prayer never leaves us without sweetness. It is honey that flows into the souls and makes all things sweet. When we pray properly, sorrows disappear like snow before the sun."

- Saint John Vianney

Prayer before Mass

Almighty and ever-living God,
I approach the sacrament
of Your only-begotten Son
Our Lord Jesus Christ,
I come sick to the doctor of life,
unclean to the fountain of mercy,
blind to the radiance of eternal light,
and poor and needy to the Lord
of heaven and earth.
Lord, in your great generosity,
heal my sickness,
wash away my defilement,
enlighten my blindness, enrich my poverty,
and clothe my nakedness.
May I receive the bread of angels,
the King of kings and Lord of lords,
with humble reverence,
with the purity and faith,
the repentance and love,
and the determined purpose
that will help to bring me to salvation.
May I receive the sacrament
of the Lord's Body and Blood,
and its reality and power.
Kind God,
may I receive the Body
of Your only-begotten Son,
our Lord Jesus Christ,
born from the womb of the Virgin Mary,
and so be received into His mystical body
and numbered among His members.
Loving Father,
as on my earthly pilgrimage
I now receive Your beloved Son
under the veil of a sacrament,
may I one day see him face to face in glory,
who lives and reigns with You forever. Amen.

Written by Saint Thomas Aquinas

Prayer for after Mass (Anima Christi)

Soul of Christ, make me holy.
Body of Christ, save me.
Blood of Christ, fill me with love.
Water from Christ's side, wash me.
Passion of Christ, strengthen me.
Good Jesus, hear me.
Within your wounds, hide me.
Never let me be parted from you.
From the evil enemy, protect me.
At the hour of my death, call me,
and tell me to come to you that with your saints I may praise you through
all eternity.
Amen.

The Penitential Psalms

Pope Innocent III (1198-1216) prescribed the recitation of the seven penitential Psalms during the season of Lent. Later on, Pope St. Pius V (1566-1572) specified their use on all of the Fridays throughout the season of Lent.

Psalm 6

2 O Lord, do not reprove me in Thy wrath, nor in Thy anger chastise me.
3 Have mercy on me, Lord, for I am weak, heal me, Lord, for my body is in torment.
4 And my soul is greatly troubled, but Thou, O Lord, how long?
5 Turn to me, O Lord, and deliver my soul; save me on account of Thy mercy.
6 For who amongst the dead remembers Thee, who of the dead will tell of Thee?
7 I have suffered and wept, every night have I washed my bed and drenched my blanket with my tears.
8 My eyes are filled with grief, I have grown feeble in the midst of my enemies.
9 Leave me, all you who do evil, for the Lord has heard the sound of my weeping.
10 The Lord has heard my appeal, the Lord has accepted my prayer.
11 May my enemies be put to shame and come to ruin. May they be turned away and be swiftly put to shame.

Psalm 31

1b Blessed is he whose iniquities are forgiven, and whose sins are covered.
2 Blessed is the man to whom the Lord hath not imputed sin, and in whose
spirit there is no guile.
3 Because I was silent my bones wasted away, as I cried out all day.
4 For day and night Thy hand was heavy upon me: I am twisted in my
affliction whilst the thorn is fastened upon me.
5 I have acknowledged my sin to Thee, and my guilt I have not concealed.
5b I said "I will confess my injustice against myself to the Lord:" and Thou
hast forgiven the wickedness of my sin.
6 For this shall every one that is holy pray to Thee in due time.
6a Though in a flood of many waters, they shall not reach him.
7 Thou art my refuge, from the tribulation which surrounds me: my joy,
deliver me from those surrounding me.
8 I will give thee understanding, and I will instruct thee in the way in which
thou shalt walk: I will fix my eyes upon thee.
9 Do not become like the horse and the mule, who have no understanding.
9a With bit and bridle bind them fast, else they will not come near to thee.
10 Many are the sorrows of the sinner, but mercy shall surround him that
hopeth in the Lord.
11 Be glad in the Lord, and rejoice, ye just, and glory, all ye of righteous
heart.

Psalm 37

2 O Lord, rebuke me not in Thy furor; nor chastise me in Thy wrath.

3 For thy arrows are fastened in me: and Thy hand hath descended upon me.

4 There is no health in my flesh in the face of Thy wrath: there is no peace for my bones in the face of my sins.

5 For my iniquities are gone over my head: and are a heavy burden too heavy to bear.

6 My wounds are putrid and corrupt, in the face of my foolishness.

7 I am miserable and am bowed down: all the day long I walked in sadness .

8 For my insides are filled with mocking; and there is no health in my flesh.

9 Greatly am I afflicted and humbled: I roared with the groaning of my heart.

10 Lord, before Thee are all my desires, and my groaning is not hidden from Thee.

11 My heart is troubled, my strength hath left me, and the light of my eyes themselves is not with me.

12 My friends and my neighbors have drawn near me and stood against me.

12a And those who were near me stood afar:

13 They laid snares, those who sought my soul.

13a And they that sought evil for me said wicked things, all day long they planned deceitful things.

14 But I, as a deaf man, heard not: and as a dumb man not opening his mouth.

15 And I became like one that heareth not: and that hath no reproofs in his mouth.

16 For in Thee, O Lord, have I hoped: Thou wilt hear me, O Lord my God.

17 For I said, "May my enemies never rejoice over me: when my feet stumble, they speak great things against me."

18 For I am ready for the whip: and my sorrow is continually before me.

19 For I will declare my inequity: and I will be sorry for my sin.

20 But my enemies live, and are stronger than I, and they that hate me wrongfully multiply.

21 They that render evil for good, have humiliated me, because I followed goodness.

22 Forsake me not, O Lord, my God, depart not from me.

23 Hasten unto my help, O Lord, God of my salvation.

Psalm 50: Miserére

Have mercy on me, O God, according to Thy great mercy; and according to the multitude of Thy tender mercies: blot out my iniquity.

4 Wash me from my iniquity; and cleanse me of my sin.

5 For I acknowledge my iniquity, and my sin is always before me.

6 Against Thee alone have I sinned and done evil in Thy sight; that Thou mayest be justified in Thy sentence and mayest overcome when judged.

7 For behold, I was conceived in sin, and in sin my mother conceived me;

8 For behold, Thou hast loved truth, and the uncertain and hidden things of Thy wisdom Thou hast shown me.

9 Thou shalt sprinkle me with hyssop, and I shall be cleansed, Thou shalt wash me, and I shall be made whiter than snow.

10 Thou shalt make me hear of joy and gladness, and the bones Thou hath crushed shall rejoice.

11 Turn away Thy face from my sins, and blot out all my iniquities.

12 Create in me a clean heart, O God, and renew a steadfast spirit within me.

13 Cast me not from Thy presence, and take not Thy holy spirit from me.

14 Restore unto me the joy of Thy salvation, and strengthen me with Thy spirit.

Psalm 101

1 A psalm for David himself. Mercy and judgment I will sing to thee, O Lord: I will sing,
2 And I will understand in the unspotted way, when thou shalt come to me. I walked in the innocence of my heart, in the midst of my house.
3 I will not set before my eyes any unjust thing: I hated the workers of iniquities.
4 The perverse heart did not cleave to me: and the malignant, that turned aside from me, I would not know.
5 The man that in private detracted his neighbour, him did I persecute. With him that had a proud eye, and an unsatiable heart, I would not eat.
6 My eyes were upon the faithful of the earth, to sit with me: the man that walked in the perfect way, he served me.
7 He that worketh pride shall not dwell in the midst of my house: he that speaketh unjust things did not prosper before my eyes.
8 In the morning I put to death all the wicked of the land: that I might cut off all the workers of iniquity from the city of the Lord.

Psalm 129: De Profundis

1 Out of the depths have I cried unto Thee, O Lord: Lord hear my voice.
2 Let Thine ears be attentive to the voice of my supplication.
3 If Thou, Lord, shouldst mark iniquities, O Lord, who shall stand?
4 But there is forgiveness with Thee: because of Thy law I wait for Thee, O Lord.
5 My soul waiteth on His word: my soul hopeth in the Lord.
6 From the morning watch even until night let Israel hope in the Lord:
7 For with the Lord there is mercy, and with Him is plentiful redemption.
8 And He shall redeem Israel, from all their iniquities.

Psalm 142

1b Hear, O Lord, my prayer, give ear to my supplication in Thy truth: hear me in Thy justice.

2 And enter not into judgment with Thy servant: for no one living shall be justified in Thy sight.

3 For the enemy hath persecuted my soul: he hath ground my life into the earth.

3b He hath made me dwell in darkness as the dead of old.

4 And my spirit is in anguish within me: my heart within me is troubled.

5 I remembered the days of old, I meditated on all Thy works: upon the works of Thy hands I pondered.

6 I stretched forth my hands to Thee: my soul is as earth without water unto Thee.

7 Hear me speedily, O Lord: my spirit hath fainted away.

7b Turn not away Thy face from me, lest I be like those that go down into the pit.

8 Cause me to hear Thy mercy in the morning; for in Thee have I hoped.

8b Make the way known to me, wherein I should walk: for I have lifted up my soul to Thee.

9 Deliver me from my enemies, O Lord, to Thee have I fled.

10 Teach me to do Thy will, for Thou art my God.

10b Thy good spirit shall lead me into the right land:

11 for Thy name's sake, O Lord, Thou wilt give me life in Thy justice.

11b Thou shalt bring my soul out of trouble.

12 And in Thy mercy Thou wilt destroy my enemies.

12b And Thou wilt cut off all that afflict my soul: for I am Thy servant.

Prayers to the Holy Spirit

"How often I failed in my duty to God, because I was not leaning on the strong pillar of prayer."

- St. Teresa of Avila

Come, Holy Spirit

Come, O Holy Spirit,
fill the hearts of your faithful
and enkindle in them the fire of your love.
Send forth your Spirit, and they shall be created.
And you shall renew the face of the earth.

Let us pray:

O God, who has taught the hearts of the faithful by the light of the Holy
Spirit,
grant that by the gift of the same Spirit
we may be always truly wise and ever rejoice in his consolation,
through Christ our Lord.
Amen.

Come, Holy Spirit, Come

Come, Holy Spirit, come,
and from your celestial home
shed a ray of light divine.
Come, Father of the poor,
Come, source of all our store.
Come, within our bosoms shine.
You, of comforters best;
You the soul's most welcome guest.
Sweet refreshment here below.
In our labor, rest most sweet;
Grateful coolness in the heat;
Solace in the midst of woe.
O most Blessed Light Divine,
shine within these hearts of thine,
and our inmost being fill.
Where you are not, man has naught.
Nothing good in deed or thought
Nothing free from taint of ill.
Heal our wounds, our strength renew;
On our dryness pour your dew;
Wash the stains of guilt away.
Bend the stubborn heart and will.
Melt the frozen, warm the chill.
Guide the steps that go astray.
On the faithful, who adore.
And confess you, evermore.
In Your sev'nfold gift descend.
Give us virtue's sure reward.
Give us your salvation, Lord.
Give us joys that never end.

Amen. (Alleluia.)

Veni Creator

Come, O Creator Spirit blest! And in our souls take up Thy rest; Come with Thy grace and heavenly aid, To fill the hearts which Thou hast made. Great Paraclete! To Thee we cry, O highest gift of God most high! O font of life! O fire of love! And sweet anointing from above.

Thou in Thy sevenfold gifts art known, The finger of God's hand we own; The promise of the Father, Thou! Who dost the tongue with power endow.

Kindle our senses from above, And make our hearts overflow with love; With patience firm and virtue high The weakness of our flesh supply.

Far from us drive the foe we dread, And grant us Thy true peace instead; So shall we not, with Thee for guide, Turn from the path of life aside.

Oh, may Thy grace on us bestow The Father and the Son to know, And Thee, through endless times confessed, Of both, the eternal Spirit blest.

All glory while the ages run Be to the Father and the Son Who rose from death; the same to Thee, O Holy Spirit, eternally.
Amen.

St. Augustine's Prayer to the Holy Spirit

Breathe in me, O Holy Spirit, that my thoughts may all be holy.
Act in me, O Holy Spirit, that my work, too, may be holy.
Draw my heart, O Holy Spirit, that I love but what is holy.
Strengthen me, O Holy Spirit, to defend all that is holy.
Guard me, then, O Holy Spirit, that I always may be holy.
Amen.

Prayers for Someone who has Passed Away

"The prayer most pleasing to God is that made for others and particularly for the poor souls. Pray for them, if you want your prayers to bring high interest."

- Blessed Anne Catherine Emmerich

Eternal Rest

Eternal rest grant unto them, O Lord,
and let perpetual light shine upon them.
May the souls of the faithful departed,
through the mercy of God,
rest in peace.
Amen.

Prayer for a Deceased One

O Lord, into your hands we commit (name).
Thoughout his/her life you showed them your love and kindness.
Now I ask that you deliver them from every evil there is and to grant them
enter eternal rest.

O Lord, the old order has truly passed away. Welcome them into your
paradise where there is no sorrow, weeping or pain. Let them feel fullness,
peace and joy with your son and the Holy Spirit, for ever and ever.
Amen.

Prayers of the Saints

"Prayer ought to be humble, fervent, resigned, persevering, and accompanied with great reverence. One should consider that he stands in the presence of a God, and speaks with a Lord before whom the angels tremble from awe and fear."
- Saint Mary Magdalen de Pazzi

Prayer of St. Francis

Lord, make me an instrument of your peace.
Where there is hatred, let me sow love,
Where there is injury, pardon
Where there is doubt, faith,
Where there is despair, hope,
Where there is darkness, light,
Where there is sadness, joy.
O Divine Master, grant that I may not so much seek to be consoled as to console, not so much to be understood as to understand, not so much to be loved, as to love; for it is in giving that we receive, it is in pardoning that we are pardoned, it is in dying that we awake to eternal life.

Prayer of St. Francis Praising Mary the Mother of Jesus

Hail, holy Lady, most holy Queen, Mary, Mother of God, ever Virgin.
You were chosen by the Most High Father in heaven, consecrated by Him, with His most Holy Beloved Son and the Holy Spirit, the Comforter.
On you descended and still remains all the fullness of grace and every good.
Hail, His Palace. Hail His Tabernacle.
Hail His Robe.
Hail His Handmaid.
Hail, His Mother.
And Hail, all holy Virtues, who, by grace and inspiration of the Holy Spirit, are poured into the hearts of the faithful so that from their faithless state, they may be made faithful servants of God through you.

Study Prayer of St. Thomas Aquinas

Creator of all things,
true Source of light and wisdom,
lofty origin of all being,
graciously let a ray of Your brilliance
penetrate into the darkness of my understanding
and take from me the double darkness
in which I have been born,
an obscurity of both sin and ignorance.
Give me a sharp sense of understanding,
a retentive memory,
and the ability to grasp things correctly and fundamentally.
Grant me the talent of being exact in my explanations,
and the ability to express myself with thoroughness and charm.
Point out the beginning,
direct the progress,
and help in completion;
through Christ our Lord.

St. Patrick's Breastplate Prayer

I bind unto myself today
The strong name of the Trinity,
By invocation of the same,
The Three in One and One in Three.

I bind this day to me forever,
By power of faith, Christ's Incarnation;
His baptism in the Jordan River;
His death on cross for my salvation;
His bursting from the spicèd tomb;
His riding up the heavenly way;
His coming at the day of doom;
I bind unto myself today.

I bind unto myself the power
Of the great love of the Cherubim;
The sweet 'Well done' in judgment hour;
The service of the Seraphim,

Confessors' faith, Apostles' word,
The Patriarchs' prayers, the Prophets' scrolls,
All good deeds done unto the Lord,
And purity of virgin souls.

I bind unto myself today
The virtues of the starlit heaven,
The glorious sun's life-giving ray,
The whiteness of the moon at even,
The flashing of the lightning free,
The whirling wind's tempestuous shocks,
The stable earth, the deep salt sea,
Around the old eternal rocks.

I bind unto myself today
The power of God to hold and lead,
His eye to watch, His might to stay,
His ear to hearken to my need.
The wisdom of my God to teach,
His hand to guide, his shield to ward,
The word of God to give me speech,
His heavenly host to be my guard.

Against the demon snares of sin,
The vice that gives temptation force,
The natural lusts that war within,
The hostile men that mar my course;
Or few or many, far or nigh,
In every place and in all hours
Against their fierce hostility,
I bind to me these holy powers.

Against all Satan's spells and wiles,
Against false words of heresy,
Against the knowledge that defiles,
Against the heart's idolatry,
Against the wizard's evil craft,
Against the death-wound and the burning
The choking wave and the poisoned shaft,
Protect me, Christ, till thy returning.

Christ be with me, Christ within me,
Christ behind me, Christ before me,

Christ beside me, Christ to win me,
Christ to comfort and restore me,
Christ beneath me, Christ above me,
Christ in quiet, Christ in danger,
Christ in hearts of all that love me,
Christ in mouth of friend and stranger.

I bind unto myself the name,
The strong name of the Trinity;
By invocation of the same.
The Three in One, and One in Three,
Of whom all nature hath creation,
Eternal Father, Spirit, Word:
Praise to the Lord of my salvation,
salvation is of Christ the Lord.

Prayer of St. Patrick
I arise today
Through the strength of heaven;
Light of the sun,
Splendor of fire,
Speed of lightning,
Swiftness of the wind,
Depth of the sea,
Stability of the earth,
Firmness of the rock.

I arise today
Through God's strength to pilot me;
God's might to uphold me,
God's wisdom to guide me,
God's eye to look before me,
God's ear to hear me,
God's word to speak for me,
God's hand to guard me,
God's way to lie before me,
God's shield to protect me,
God's hosts to save me
Afar and anear,
Alone or in a mulitude.
Christ shield me today
Against wounding
Christ with me, Christ before me, Christ behind me,

Christ in me, Christ beneath me, Christ above me,
Christ on my right, Christ on my left,
Christ when I lie down, Christ when I sit down,
Christ in the heart of everyone who thinks of me,
Christ in the mouth of everyone who speaks of me,
Christ in the eye that sees me,
Christ in the ear that hears me.
I arise today
Through the mighty strength
Of the Lord of creation.

Prayer of St. Patrick For The Faithful
May the Strength of God guide us.
May the Power of God preserve us.
May the Wisdom of God instruct us.
May the Hand of God protect us.
May the Way of God direct us.
May the Shield of God defend us.
May the Angels of God guard us,
Against the snares of the evil one.

May Christ be with us!
May Christ be before us!
May Christ be in us,
Christ be over all!

May Thy Grace, Lord,
Always be ours,
This day, O Lord, and forevermore.

Amen.

Prayer of St. Anselm

O Lord my God,
Teach my heart this day where and how to see you,
Where and how to find you.
You have made me and remade me,
And you have bestowed on me
All the good things I possess,
And still I do not know you.
I have not yet done that
For which I was made.
Teach me to seek you,
For I cannot seek you
Unless you teach me,
Or find you
Unless you show yourself to me.
Let me seek you in my desire,
Let me desire you in my seeking.
Let me find you by loving you,
Let me love you when I find you.

Prayer of St. Francis of Assissi

You are holy, Lord, the only God,
and Your deeds are wonderful.
You are strong.
You are great.
You are the Most High.
You are Almighty.
You, Holy Father are King of heaven and earth.
You are Three and One, Lord God, all Good.
You are Good, all Good, supreme Good,
Lord God, living and true.
You are love. You are wisdom.
You are humility. You are endurance.
You are rest. You are peace.
You are joy and gladness.
You are justice and moderation.
You are all our riches, and You suffice for us.
You are beauty.
You are gentleness.
You are our protector.
You are our guardian and defender.
You are our courage. You are our haven and our hope.
You are our faith, our great consolation.
You are our eternal life, Great and Wonderful Lord,
God Almighty, Merciful Saviour.

Canticle of the Sun by St. Francis of Assisi

Be praised, my Lord,
For all your creatures,
And first for brother sun,
Who makes the day bright and luminous.
He is beautiful and radiant
With great splendor
He is the image of You,
Most high.
Be praised, my Lord,
For sister moon and the stars.
You placed them in the sky,
So bright and twinkling.

Prayer of St. Ethelwold

May God the Father bless us,
may Christ take care of us,
the Holy Ghost enlighten us all the days of our life.
The Lord be our defender and keeper of body and soul,
both now and forever, to the ages of ages.

Prayer of St. Columba

Alone with none but thee, my God,
I journey on my way.
What need I fear when thou art near,
Oh king of night and day?
More safe am I within thy hand
Than if a host did round me stand.

Prayer of St. Gregory

It is only right, with all the powers of our heart and mind, to praise You
Father and Your Only-Begotten Son, Our Lord Jesus Christ.
Dear Father, by Your wondrous condescension of Loving-Kindness toward
us, Your servants, You gave up Your Son.

Dear Jesus You paid the debt of Adam for us to the Eternal Father by Your Blood poured forth in Loving-Kindness.

You cleared away the darkness of sin by Your magnificent and radiant Resurrection.

You broke the bonds of death and rose from the grave as a Conqueror.

You reconciled Heaven and earth. Our life had no hope of Eternal Happiness before You redeemed us.

Your Resurrection has washed away our sins, restored our innocence and brought us joy.

How inestimable is the tenderness of Your Love!

We pray You, Lord, to preserve Your servants in the peaceful enjoyment of this Easter happiness.

We ask this through Jesus Christ Our Lord, Who lives and reigns with God The Father, in the unity of the Holy Spirit, forever and ever.

Amen.

Prayer of St. Augustine

Lord Jesus, let me know myself and know Thee,
And desire nothing save only Thee.
Let me hate myself and love Thee.
Let me do everything for the sake of Thee.
Let me humble myself and exalt Thee.
Let me think nothing except Thee.
Let me die to myself and live in Thee.
Let me accept whatever happens as from Thee.
Let me banish self and follow Thee,
and ever desire to follow Thee.
Let me fly from myself and take refuge in Thee,
that I may deserve to be defended by Thee.
Let me fear for myself, let me fear Thee,
and let me be among those who are chosen by Thee.
Let me distrust myself and put my trust in Thee.
Let me be willing to obey for the sake of Thee.
Let me cling to nothing save only to Thee,
and let me be poor because of Thee.
Look upon me, that I may love Thee.
Call me that I may see Thee,
And forever enjoy Thee.

Holy Spirit Prayer of Saint Augustine

Breathe in me, O Holy Spirit,
That my thoughts may all be holy.
Act in me, O Holy Spirit,
That my work, too, may be holy.
Draw my heart, O Holy Spirit,
That I love but what is holy.
Strengthen me, O Holy Spirit,
To defend all that is holy.
Guard me, then, O Holy Spirit,
That I always may be holy.

Second Prayer of St. Augustine: Act of Hope

By Saint Augustine of Hippo.

For Your mercies' sake, O Lord my God,
tell me what You are to me.
Say to my soul: "I am your salvation."
So speak that I may hear, O Lord;
my heart is listening;
open it that it may hear You,
and say to my soul: "I am your salvation."
After hearing this word,
may I come in haste to take hold of you.
Hide not Your face from me.
Let me see Your face even if I die,
lest I die with longing to see it.
The house of my soul is too small to receive You;
let it be enlarged by You.
It is all in ruins;
do You repair it.
There are thing in it,
I confess and I know,
that must offend Your sight.
But who shall cleanse it?
Or to what others besides You shall I cry out?
From my secret sins cleanse me, O Lord,
and from those of others spare your servant.
Amen.

You Are Christ

A Prayer of St. Augustine of Hippo

You are Christ,
my Holy Father,
my Tender God,
my Great King,
my Good Shepherd,
my Only Master,
my Best Helper,
my Most Beautiful and my Beloved,
my Living Bread,
my Priest Forever,
my Leader to my Country,
my True Light,
my Holy Sweetness,
my Straight Way,
my Excellent Wisdom,
my Pure Simplicity,
my Peaceful Harmony,
my Entire Protection,
my Good Portion,
my Everlasting Salvation.
Christ Jesus, Sweet Lord,
why have I ever loved,
why in my whole life
have I ever desired anything except You,
Jesus my God?
Where was I when I was not in spirit with You?
Now, from this time forth,
do you, all my desires, grow hot,
and flow out upon the Lord Jesus:
run... you have been tardy until now;
hasten where you are going;
seek Whom you are seeking.
O, Jesus may he who loves You
not be an anathema;
may he who loves You
not be filled with bitterness.
O, Sweet Jesus,
may every good feeling that is fitted for Your praise,

love You, delight in You, adore You!
God of my heart,
and my Portion, Christ Jesus,
may my heart faint away in spirit,
and may You be my Life within me!
May the live coal of Your Love
grow hot within my spirit
and break forth into a perfect fire;
may it burn incessantly on the altar of my heart;
may it glow in my innermost being;
may it blaze in hidden recesses of my soul;
and in the days of my consummation
may I be found consummated with You!
Amen.

Prayer of St. Ignatius of Loyola

Dearest Lord, teach me to be generous;
Teach me to serve thee as thou deservest;
To give and not to count the cost,
To fight and not to seek for rest,
To labour and not to seek reward,
Save that of knowing that I do thy will.

Suscipe of St. Ignatius of Loyola

Take, Lord, and receive all my liberty,
my memory, my understanding,
and my entire will,
All I have and call my own.

You have given all to me.
To you, Lord, I return it.

Everything is yours; do with it what you will.
Give me only your love and your grace,
that is enough for me.

Prayer of St. Teresa Of Avila

Govern everything by your wisdom, O Lord, so that my soul may always be serving you
in the way you will
and not as I choose.
Let me die to myself so that I may serve you;
let me live to you who are life itself.
Amen.

Prayer of Saint Richard of Chichester

Thanks be to thee, my Lord Jesus Christ,
for all the benefits thou hast given me,
for all the pains and insults thou hast borne for me.
O most merciful redeemer, friend and brother,
may I know thee more clearly,
love thee more dearly,
and follow thee more nearly, day by day.
Amen.

A Morning Prayer written by St. Therese

O my God! I offer Thee all my actions of this day for the intentions and for the glory of the Sacred Heart of Jesus. I desire to sanctify every beat of my heart, my every thought, my simplest works, by uniting them to Its infinite merits; and I wish to make reparation for my sins by casting them into the furnace of Its Merciful Love. O my God! I ask of Thee for myself and for those whom I hold dear, the grace to fulfill perfectly Thy Holy Will, to accept for love of Thee the joys and sorrows of this passing life, so that we may one day be united together in heaven for all Eternity.
Amen.

Prayer of St. Thomas Aquinas

O God, who in this wondrous sacrament hast left unto us a memorial of
thy passion;
grant us so to venerate the sacred mysteries of thy body and blood,
that we may ever continue to feel within ourselves the blessed fruit of thy
redemption.
Who livest and reignest God, for ever and ever.

Prayer of St. Ignatius Loyola

Dearest Lord,
teach me to be generous;
teach me to serve You as You deserve;
to give and not to count the cost,
to fight and not to heed the wounds,
to toil and not to seek for rest,
to labour and not to ask for reward
save that of knowing I am doing Your Will.

Prayers to the Saints

"We must pray without ceasing, in every occurrence and employment of our lives - that prayer which is rather a habit of lifting up the heart to God as in a constant communication with Him."
- St. Elizabeth Ann Seton

Prayer of Children to St. Nicholas

God Our Father we pray,
That through the Intercessory of St. Nicholas,
You will protect our children.
Keep them safe from harm,
And help them grow,
And become worthy of Your sight.

Give them strength,
To keep their Faith in You,
And to keep alive their joy,
In Your creation.
Through Jesus Christ Our Lord.

Amen.

Special Need Prayer to St. Rita

O powerful St. Rita,
rightly called Saint of the Impossible,
I come to you with confidence in my great need.
You know well my trials,
for you yourself were many times burdened in this life.
Come to my help,
speak for me,
pray with me,
intercede on my behalf before the Father.
I know that God has a most generous heart
and that he is a most loving Father.
Join your prayers to mine
and obtain for me the grace I desire
(Make your request...)
You who were so very pleasing to God on earth
and are so much so now in heaven,
I promise to use this favor, when granted,
to better my life,
to proclaim God's mercy,
and to make you more widely known and loved.
Amen.

Prayer to St. Anthony (for lost or missing items)

O Blessed Apostle St. Anthony,
By the grace of God you have been made a powerful advocate for the restoring of things that have been lost or stolen.

I turn to you now, imploring you with childlike love and confidence.
You have helped many before me, many children of God and I know that you can help me as well.

O gentle and loving St Anthony, who was chosen by God as a vessel for his miracles, whisper my petition into the ears of the sweet infant Jesus and the gratitude of my heart will forever be yours.

A Prayer to St. Gerard (for Motherhood)

O glorious Saint Gerard,
powerful intercessor before God,
and wonder worker of our day,
I call upon you and seek your help.
You who always fulfilled God's will on earth,
help me to do God's holy will.
Intercede with the Giver of life,
from whom all parenthood proceeds,
that I may conceive and raise children who will please God in this life,
and be heirs to the kingdom of heaven.
Amen.

Prayer to St. Christopher (whilst travelling)

St Christopher, protect me today and I travel the road along my way.
Show me a warning sign when danger is near, so that I may stop while the passing is clear.
Carry me safely to my place I am going,
In your safety and protection all the knowing.
In your power and safety I trust,
Myself and my possessions as I know I must. Amen.

Prayer to St. Christopher for Motorists

Dear Saint Christopher,
Protect me today
in all of my travels
along the roads way.

Give your warning sign
if danger is near
so that I may stop
while the path is clear.

Be at my window
and direct me through
when the vision blurs from out of the blue.

Carry me safely
to my destined place,
like you carried Christ
in your close embrace.

Amen.

Prayer to St. Jude (For Lost Causes)

O most holy apostle and faithful servant of Jesus, I pray to you St. Jude.
You are the patron saint of lost and hopeless causes, of all things we despair
of.
Pray for me for I am suffering and I too have a lost cause.
(State your request here)
Come to my assistance in this hour of need and grant the help of heaven
and everything above in getting me though this time.

Amen.

Printed in Great Britain
by Amazon

80052702R00050